Coast to Coast with a Camera

The Journey in Pictures

DAVID SHAW

Love from

Angela x

HAYLOFT
KIRKBY STEPHEN

First published by Hayloft 2011

Hayloft Publishing Ltd, South Stainmore,
Kirkby Stephen, Cumbria, CA17 4DJ

tel: 07971 352473
email: books@hayloft.eu
web: www.hayloft.eu

ISBN 1 904524 83 4

CAP data for this title are available from the British Library

Designed, printed and bound in the EU

Papers used by Hayloft are natural, recyclable products made from wood grown in sustainable forests.
The manufacturing processes conform to the environmental regulations of the country of origin.

This book is dedicated to the craftsmen:

the farmers, quarrymen, lead miners, builders of stone walls and all others who sculpted this landscape,
the results, though not always picturesque, bear testimony to their labour.

The Irish Sea in truculent mood.

CONTENTS

A wild day in Ennerdale, looking towards Bowness Point and Pillar.

East Gill Force, Swaledale.

INTRODUCTION

In 1972 Alfred Wainwright, universally known as *AW,* completed his coast to coast walk; a journey of 190 miles across northern England from St. Bees in the west to Robin Hood's Bay in the east. It is a masterly route, linking the Lake District, Yorkshire Dales and North Yorkshire Moors National Parks. Nevertheless, *AW* was at pains to establish that this was **A** coast to coast walk, not **THE** coast to coast walk, and encouraged prospective walkers to vary the expedition at will to include places of individual interest.

AW wrote, "One should always have a definite objective, in a walk, as in life - it is so much more satisfying to reach a target by personal effort than to wander aimlessly." His objective, and that of those who followed his lead, was to walk the breadth of England. I freely admit that I did not do the whole coast to coast walk in one go, but some sections I walked several times in order to capture photographs under the best weather conditions. I have also taken *AW* at his word and included some exploratory deviations, Borrowdale for example, is not really included in the walk but who, visiting Cumbria, could resist taking a peek at this most beautiful Lakeland valley?

And so, without more ado, let's baptise the boots in the Irish Sea and set out to fulfil a personal ambition, whatever that ambition may be.

The West Door, Priory Church

ST. BEES TO ENNERDALE BRIDGE

The village of St. Bees lies four miles to the south of Whitehaven and can trace its history back to Roman times when fortifications protected the coast from marauding Scots and Irish. Two notable institutions grace St. Bees, namely the Priory Church, dedicated to St. Mary and St. Bega and the Grammar School, founded in 1583 by the Archbishop of Canterbury, Edmund Grindal.

Legend has it that St. Bega escaped an arranged marriage in Ireland and landed here in the 7th century whereupon she begged the local landowner for land to build a nunnery. He graciously granted her all land covered in snow on the following day, as it was Midsummer's eve, he must have felt it was a good bet. Due to Divine intervention or a freak weather pattern, three miles of land around the headland was covered in snow on the next day and the nunnery was established. This was succeeded in the 12th century by a small Benedictine monastery which survived until Henry VIII decreed the Dissolution of the Monasteries in the 16th century. In 1817 a college to train clergy, the first other than Oxford and Cambridge, was set up within the Priory.

During excavations in the chancel in 1981 the skeleton of a female was found close to a lead coffin containing the body of a man wrapped in cloth impregnated with bees wax. A subsequent autopsy revealed that the body was around 500 years old and remarkably well preserved, with much soft tissue and even liquid blood remaining. The body was re-buried in the chancel aisle.

The church is of mixed architectural styles ranging from Norman through Early English to Gothic. Among its attributes are the tower which houses a ring of eight bells and a fine Henry Willis organ which was completed in 1899.

Anyway, enough history for the moment, the idea is to walk across England from west to east, with the wind

The Priory Church of St. Mary and St. Bega.

behind us, though paradoxically the initial direction is north rather than east. The route has been described by its originator in far greater detail than I can hope to achieve so I'll limit myself to providing the pictures and suitable captions - just turn right at the caravans and follow the cliff.

Approximately half way between South Head and North Head lies Fleswick Bay. The shingle beach can be

The South Head.

Fleswick Bay.

reached by means of a simple scramble down the cliff to view the rock scenery, caves and flowers clinging tenaciously to the near vertical rock face.

Without the warning provided by a lighthouse, the cliffs around St. Bees posed a danger to small vessels trading along the coast between the ports of Wales and the Solway Firth. The first lighthouse was built in 1718 and operated by Thomas Lutwige who was charged an annual rent of £20. To recoup his costs, and hopefully make a profit, dues were charged at the rate of 1.5 old pence (just

11

over ½ p) per ton on cargo carried by ships calling at Whitehaven, Maryport and Workington. The original tower was nine metres high and five metres in diameter with the light being provided from a small grate of burning coal at the top.

North Head

St. Bees Lighthouse

In 1822 the tower was destroyed by fire and replaced by the present structure which was then fuelled by oil. The lighthouse was automated in 1987 and is now powered by a 1,500 watt lamp emitting two white flashes every twenty seconds. The range of the light is 21 nautical miles.

There is a choice of routes from the lighthouse. The lane passing Tarnflat Hall may be taken directly to Sandwith or, perhaps better in good weather, the coastal path with its views of Saltom Bay can be followed, passing Birkhams Quarry where red sandstone is extracted by seemingly precariously balanced machinery.

Either route will lead the walker to the charming village of Sandwith, once a centre for the mining of anhydrite (gypsum) which was used by the Marchon Chemical Company in nearby Whitehaven. The mineral was used in the production of sulphuric acid and hence phosphoric

Saltom Bay and Whitehaven.

Sandwith.

acid which is an essential ingredient in the manufacture of detergents and cleaning products. The Sandwith plant opened in 1955 and at its peak in 1968 was producing 350,000 tons of sulphuric acid, 165,000 tons of phosphoric acid and 350,000 tons of cement per annum. In the early 1970s it became more economic to import sulphur as a raw material and production of sulphuric acid ceased in 1976 followed by the closure of the phosphoric acid plant in 1992.

This marked the end of large scale mineral extraction in western Cumbria. Coal mining started in the thirteenth century when monks from St. Bees supervised mining at Arrowthwaite and ended with the closure of the Haig Pit near Whitehaven in 1986. The rich red colour of the local sandstone testifies to the presence of iron ore (haematite), which is still mined to a small extent, at the Florence Mine near Egremont.

Fortunately other industries have moved into the region to provide much needed employment, the nuclear facility at Sellafield being by far the largest and most important. Activity at the site began in 1955 with the construction of the world's first nuclear power station, Calder Hall, which was opened by the Queen in October 1956, heralding an era when electricity would be 'too cheap to meter.' Of course, in truth, activity at the site had little to do with the generation of electricity and a lot to do with the production of weapons grade plutonium neded to keep pace with developments in the USA and the then USSR. Calder Hall power station closed in 2003, its output of 196 megawatts being considered too puny for modern demands.

Today the site extends to approximately four square kilometres and employs 10,000 workers. Its function, to quote the podcast, is: "In addition to the remediation, decommissioning and clean-up of the historic legacy, we recycle used fuel from nuclear power stations, manufacture Mixed Oxide Fuel, safely manage and store nuclear materials and process and store low, intermediate and high level nuclear wastes." Sellafield Ltd claims to have the largest concentration of nuclear expertise in Europe to accomplish its duties. Let's hope they are right!

Some say that nuclear power is a pact with the devil; if this is the case then Satan has certainly kept his side of the bargain, without it West Cumbria would be a far more impoverished place.

Sellafield.

From Sandwith the route continues on a mixture of roads, tracks and field paths via the village of Moor Row with retrospective views of the West Cumbria plain to arrive at Cleator. This village, along with its partner Cleator Moor, also owes its existence to the mining of iron ore. Extensive rail links were constructed to transport the ore from the locality to the port of Whitehaven, these disused tracks now form part of the C2C (Coast to Coast) cycle network.

In his *Pictorial Guide*, Wainwright includes a drawing of the parish church of St. Leonard parts of which date back to the twelfth century. In the interests of balance and church unity I have chosen to add a photograph of the Roman Catholic Church of St. Mary which was opened in 1872. Although lacking the antiquity of St. Leonard's, the church has the distinction of being designed by E. W. Pugin, son of A. W. N. Pugin, the noted designer and architect perhaps best remembered for his work on the Palace of Westminster (Houses of Parliament). The Palace was built under the direction of Sir Charles Barry, but the elder Pugin was responsible for every aspect of the interiors as well as creating engineering drawings of all exterior details.

West Cumbria Plain and, right, St. Mary's Church, Cleator.

Cleator marks the end of industrialised West Cumbria and the entry to the fells of the Lake District. The little hill of Dent is traversed before descending into Uldale and subsequently Nannycatch. Here Raven Crag provides the first sight of Lakeland volcanic rock.

The path follows Nannycatch Beck upstream past Raven Crag and Flat Fell screes to join the Calder Bridge to Ennerdale Bridge road at Kinniside Stone Circle. The circle comprises eleven stones, the tallest of which is 1.5 meters in height, arranged in an eighteen metre diameter

Uldale

Nannycatch, left, and Raven Crag, above.

circle. The bases of some of the stones are set in concrete, a building material not often used by prehistoric man and sources differ on its authenticity. Some hold that the circle is composed of original stones that had been removed by local farmers and subsequently recovered to allow restoration while others maintain that the stones were arranged by a local archaeologist merely as an example of a prehistoric circle. If ther latter is true, it begs the question 'why bother?' since there are about 50 genuine stone circles in Cumbria alone.

Kinniside Stone Circle

From the stone circle it is an easy down hill stroll to the village of Ennerdale Bridge but take care on the road, it is surprisingly busy at certain times being used, one suspects as a rat run by workers from Sellafield. The village, largely composed of modern dwellings sits on the River Ehan which escapes from Ennerdale Water about a mile away, and boasts two hotels, the Shepherds Arms and the Fox and Hounds. The school survives in the centre of the village and the spiritual needs of the community are catered for by the parish church of St. Mary which nestles in the church yard close to the river.

Ennerdale Bridge

Ennerdale.

ENNERDALE BRIDGE TO ROSTHWAITE

Ennerdale is the most westerly of the Lake District valleys and, in some ways, the least developed. You will not find hotels, camp sites, ice cream shops or even a driveable road. You will find spectacular mountain scenery, a sense of solitude and an awful lot of trees. Afforestation began in 1926 and was completed around 1950; the species planted include Norway and Sitka spruce and European and Japanese larch. The Forestry Commission faced criticism over its policy of planting trees in unnatural straight lines, a practice which has since been abandoned in the Lake District.

Roe deer and red squirrel populate the forest and the surrounding crags are home to peregrine falcon, raven and buzzard. The gold crest, Britain's smallest bird, live in the area but are rarely seen, preferring to remain in the tree tops away from curious visitors.

Ennerdale, in common with most other Lakeland valleys, is the product of retreating glaciers which covered the region during the last Ice Age. The lake, Ennerdale Water, is fed by the River Liza which drains the Great Gable-Kirk Fell massif, and is noted for the purity of its water which it unobtrusively supplies to West Cumbria.

The Coast to Coast route leaves Ennerdale Bridge on the Croasdale road, turning right after about half a mile, to cross the River Ehan at its outfall from the lake, and follows a path past the pumping station along the south shore. The outcrop of Angler's Crag initially dominates the scene, while Crag Fell Pinnacles high above the path provide geological interest.

The track along the base of the crag, once considered too rough to be a walking route, climbs and descends amost to lake level between rocky outcrops, passing a feature known as Robin Hood's chair which frames a view of Pillar and the head of the valley.

Then follows a simple walk along the lake side path,

Angler's Crag.

Pictured left, Pillar from Robin Hood's Chair and below from How Hall

wet in places, before a green path leads to a footbridge over the River Liza and the forest road beyond. No one, except perhaps a fanatical arborealist, could describe the next three miles or so as inspiring, Wainwright himself says, "just keep plodding along the forest road." However, things may improve. The Wild Ennerdale Partnership, a coalition of the Forestry Commission, the National Trust and United Utilities, plan to "allow the evolution of Ennerdale as a wild valley for the benefit of people relying on natural processes to shape its landscape and ecology." If this means felling a few thousand trees and letting some daylight into the valley bottom, then it is to be applauded, but action on an industrial scale is required, in the author's humble opinion, if Ennerdale is to look like a Lake District valley again.

"Keep on plodding along the forest road..."

The road passes Low Gillerthwaite, a field study centre, Gillerthwaite Youth Hostel and High Gillerthwaite Farm and eventually emerges into daylight close to Black Sail Hut. This hut was originally a shepherd's bothy and is now probably the most isolated Youth Hostel in Britain. From here a steep path alongside Loft Beck leads to the open fell close to the Brandreth fence and the track to Honister. An alternative route, for supermen/women only, is the ascent of High Stile and the traverse of High Crag and Haystacks. Spectacular mountain views amply compensate for the extra effort involved.

Looking back to Pillar and Ennerdale.

High Crag from Haystacks.

Great Gable from Innominate Tarn.

Haystacks was a great favourite of Wainwright. He said that it, "stands unabashed and unashamed in the midst of a circle of much loftier fells, like a shaggy terrier in the company of foxhounds," only its lack of altitude excludes it from his finest half dozen but he waxes lyrical on its serpentine trails, tarns and crags. *AW's* ashes were scattered at Innominate Tarn at his own request.

The route continues along the ridge of Haystacks

Haystacks.

Buttermere and Crummock Water.

passing Blackbeck Tarn, before losing and regaining altitude to ascend Green Crag. Spectacular views of the Buttermere valley are obtained before descending to Dubs Bottom and the path to Honister.

The summit of Honister Pass is dominated by the workings of the slate mines. Here on both sides of the

Honister Crag

valley is evidence of a long history of quarrying to win green slate from the labyrinth of tunnels and levels which honeycomb the surrounding fells. Some sources claim that mining activities began here in Roman times, and certainly by the fourteenth century the industry was well established.

At this time the only way of transporting slate to the coast was by pack ponies across the high fells. The route, known as Moses Trod was named after the legendary Moses Rigg who, rather than return with empty panniers, brought smuggled whisky back to Honister. It is still in use today as a walkers' highway, and takes the easiest way possible across the slopes of Brandreth, Great Gable and Kirk Fell to arrive at Wasdale Head from where primitive roads were followed to the port of Ravenglass.

By the mid-eighteenth century road communications had improved sufficiently to allow the use of hand sledges to transport slate from the high quarries to the road head. The sledges, guided by a barrow man who ran in front, held about one third of a ton of slate and ran on artificial scree slopes to the road side. Once unloaded the barrow man would carry his sledge back up the slope. The fittest men would do this fifteen times a day.

The nineteenth and twentieth centuries saw the development of a railway system linking the mines to cutting sheds and a new road to Seatoller. The railway, in its turn, was replaced by aerial ropeways and the motor vehicles in use today. While still producing slate, today Honister is also a tourist attraction where visitors can explore the workings under supervision and enjoy the thrills of the Via Ferrata, an aerial ropeway across the face of the crag.

The old toll road leads from Honister to Seatoller and avoids the traffic of the main pass. From Seatoller the route follows the River Derwent through Johnny's Wood past Longthwaite Youth Hostel and via field paths to Rosthwaite where accommodation and refreshment can be obtained.

Seatoller.

Rosthwaite and below Stonethwaite

ROSTHWAITE TO PATTERDALE

The Coast to Coast walk makes little incursion into Borrowdale but, given that the valley runs roughly south to north, and the Coast to Coast route is west to east, this is hardly surprising. Even the inclusion of Rosthwaite is something of a diversion - it would be more direct to access Stonethwaite and Greenup Gill from Seatoller without taking the path through Johnny's Wood. This is in no way a slur on Rosthwaite which is a charming hamlet and always worthy of a visit. After the journey from Ennerdale, it is likely that accommodation and refreshment will be required. Rosthwaite provides both in abundance with three hostels, numerous B&Bs, campsites and the nearby youth hostel all offering the visitor a bed for the night in varying levels of luxury - just make sure you book in advance.

The route leaves Rosthwaite at the northern end of the village, crossing the bridge near Hazel Bank and turning right along a path following Stonethwaite Beck. The beck may be a gentle stream or a raging torrent, depending on how much of Borrowdale's considerable precipitation has recently occurred.

Although the Coast to Coast walk doesn't really visit Borrowdale, the Coast to Coast walker, if time permits, should. Borrowdale is special. A few pictures are included to whet the appetite.

Ashness Bridge and Skiddaw.

Lodore Cascade

Towards Dale Head

Derwentwater and Castle Crag.

Eagle Crag.

Eagle Crag stands at the junction of two valleys and dominates the scene on the approach to Stonethwaite. Ahead is Greenup Gill, the way to Grasmere and to the right is Langstrath with Bowfell at its head. The route does not visit Stonethwaite but prefers to remain on the other side of the beck; a footbridge provides access to waterfalls and deep crystal clear pools in a sylvan setting popular with swimmers on hot summer days.

The good track alongside Greenup Gill leads to Greenup Edge, the summit of the pass between Borrowdale and Grasmere and, in due course, to the head of Far Easdale. From here a choice of routes is available before the descent into the picturesque (and busy) village of Grasmere made famous by the poet William Wordsworth, whose grave in the churchyard of the thirteenth century St. Oswald's Church attracts many visitors.

Waterfalls on Stonethwaite Beck.

The direct route to Grasmere from the summit of Greenup Edge descends into Far Easdale and follows Easdale Gill unerringly into the village, by way of Goody Bridge. The alternative, and much to be preferred way, is a ridge walk over Calf Crag, Gibson Knott and Helm Crag.

The Head of Far Easdale.

Gibson Knott looking towards Calf Crag.

Even by Lake District standards, Helm Crag, at 1,299 feet cannot be considered a giant, but its fine summit ridge and wide ranging views make it a delectable place to be. Fairfield to the north east is seen to advantage and across Easdale Tarn, Pavey Ark, Harrison Stickle and Crinkle Crags complete the western panorama.

Helm Crag, universally known as 'The Lion and the Lamb' rises abruptly from the vale of Grasmere and owes its pet name to the resemblance of the summit rocks to Leo and his companion which crown the southern end of the summit ridge. The northern end of the rigde is similarly adorned with an outcrop of naked rock variously known as the Howitzer, the Lion Counchant and the Old Woman Playing the Organ.

Two views of the Howitzer.

Langdale Pikes across Easdale Tarn.

Above, the Lion and the Lamb; above right, Seat Sandal and below right, Fairfield, south westerly panorama.

The path descends from the summit, easily at first with fine views of Grasmere, and then more steeply to join the road leading to Goody Bridge and Grasmere village.

Grasmere, Helm Crag and St. Oswald's Church.

The path to Grisedale Tarn and hence to Patterdale leaves the Keswick to Grasmere road at Mill Bridge, a few hundred metres north of the Travellers Rest Inn and climbs past Tongue Gill Force to a gate and sheepfold close to an abandoned reservoir. There is a choice of paths here: the one to the right is shorter and easier than the left fork and appears to be the preferred route to the head of the pass. Restrospective views of the Langdale Pikes over Helm Crag provide a good excuse for frequent rests.

The path climbs steadily between Seat Sandal and

Helm Crag and the Langdales.

Fairfield to arrive at Grisedale Tarn at an altitude of 1,768 feet. There is a choice of three routes from the tarn. The direct route roughly follows Grisedale Beck from the outfall of the tarn uneventfully down to Patterdale. The St. Sunday Crag alternative goes off to the right, and the Helvellyn route climbs the slope of Dollywaggon Pike to the left. Under the conditions shown in this photograph, there is only one sensible choice.

In his pictorial guide to *A Coast to Coast Walk,* Wainwright advises that, "Before proceeding beyond the

Grisedale Tarn.

Dollywaggon Pike and below St. Sunday Crag.

tarn, sit down awhile and consult (a) the weather, (b) the time, (c) the state of the blisters and (d) the note on page 34." The note describes the Helvellyn and St. Sunday Crag alternatives. The former adds two miles and an extra 1,500 feet of ascent to the journey but rewards the walker with extensive views from the summit (depending on the weather) and an exciting traverse of Striding Edge, the finest ridge in the Lake District but, a word of caution, in icy conditions, or when it's blowing a gale, the edge is best avoided. The ascent of Helvellyn is not direct; Dollywaggon Pike (2,810 feet) and Nethermost Pike (2,920 feet) are climbed before arriving at the summit, from which the Striding Edge path leads down through the "Hole in the Wall" to Birkhouse Moor and Patterdale.

The St. Sunday Crag alternative, which adds an extra 1,000 feet and an hour to the journey, leaves the tarn and heads across pathless marshy (when it's not frozen) ground to Deepdale Hause, the depression between Fairfield and St. Sunday Crag. A line of cairns leads to a good path along the summit ridge. The route descends towards an outcrop of rock with a classic view of Ullswater and thence across the slopes of Birks to join the Grisedale road.

Of the two alternatives *AW* favours the latter, describing St. Sunday Cras as a connoisseur's mountain, lovely to walk on, quiet and free from crowds and their attendant litter.

St. Patrick's Church.

PATTERDALE TO SHAP

Patterdale takes its name from St. Patrick who is supposed to have preached in the Ullswater area around about 450AD after being shipwrecked on the Duddon Sands. Nearby at Glenridding is St. Patrick's Well, a holy well reputed to cure sickness, in which the saint baptised converts to Christianity. The church, dedicated to St. Patrick, was designed by the famous architect Anthony Salvin, and was built in 1853 to replace a fourteenth century chapel. Salvin was a student of John Nash and became an authority on medieval architecture, particularly fortifications. Among his achievements are the restoration of Windsor Castle and the Jewel House at the Tower of London.

Apart from tourism, the main industry in the valley is sheep farming but this was not always the case. Lead mining began in the seventeenth century when the Greenside Mine was opened in 1650 and continued until extraction of the ore became uneconomic leading to its closure in 1960.

Ullswater is often described as the most beautiful of lakes, nestling as it does between the Helvellyn massif to the west and the Place Fell group in the east. Every variety of Lakeland scenery is here - mature woodland leads to heather clad slopes, soaring crags and lofty mountains.

In common with Borrowdale, the Coast to Coast walk does not seek to explore the Ullswater valley to any great extent. Of course, this is entirely reasonable, since the

The head of Ullswater.

object of the exercise is to traverse northern England an reach Robin Hood's Bay, rather than dally around looking at every scenic attraction. However, since this is a more leisurely excursion with a camera (and being loath to miss the chance) I will take the opportunity to include a few more pictures.

After Patterdale the next objective is Boredale Hause which is reached by taking the lower path of two from the valley floor, accessed either through the yard of Side Farm, or from the charming cottages at Rooking, depending on where you leave the village. The track then traverses the fell side, with fine retrospective views of Place Fell to pass beneath Angle Tarn Pikes to arrive at Angle Tarn.

Looking across Ullswater towards Sandwick.

Aira Force.

Rainbow over Gowbarrow.

Angle Tarn.

On leaving Angle Tarn the path continues past Satura Crag and climbs the steep flank of he Knott ultimately leading to the summit of Kidsty Pike, the highest point reached on the Coast to Coast. The gradient gives ample excuse to pause and admire retrospective views of the Helvellyn range.

51

Part of the Helvellyn Range and Brothers Water.

A Helvellyn panorama.

The hamlet glimpsed below is Hartsop; the tarn is Hayeswater, a reservoir.

Hartsop, left, and Hayeswater, above.

Haweswater sometimes receives a bad press, not least from *AW* because of the ugly "tide mark" which appears when the water level is low. However, now that the reservoir is more sympathetically managed, the impact is much less and Haweswater is as attractive as any other Lakeland water.

Kidsty Pike and Riggindale.

Haweswater.

Departure from Haweswater also marks the departure from Lakeland, the way ahead via Burn Banks and Haweswater Beck leads to Shap passing the abbey along the way.

Shap Abbey.

56

Market Hall, Shap.

Shap Abbey, dedicated to St. Mary Magdalene, nestles in a bend of the River Lowther a mile outside the village. It was founded in 1199 by members of the Premonstratensian order, also known as the White Canons, from northern France. Most buildings date from the thirteenth century but the tower, still intact apart from its parapets and windows, is later being of sixteenth (some sources say fifteenth) century origin. Remains of the chapter house, dormitory, warming house (the only heated room), and cloisters can still be traced on the ground. The abbey was the last to fall victim of the dissolution of the monasteries by Henry VIII in 1540. Demoliton began almost immediately, with lead removed from the roofs and stone being taken away to be used for other building projects, including the Market Hall (pictured above) and Lowther Castle, near Askham.

The village of Shap straddles the A6 which was once the main west coast route to Scotland, until it was superseded by the M6 in 1970. The name still conjures up images of horrific road accidents and perilous journeys through snow drifts over Shap Summit, which at 1,400 feet makes the A6 the highest major road in England. The coming of the motorway brought peace to Shap but also sounded the death knell to many local businesses which relied on the passing traffic for their livelihood. However, all is not lost. Hotels, bed and breakfasts, and self catering cottages provide accommodation for tourists on this eastern fringe of the Lake District. Leisure activities range from bell ringing to swimming in the highest outdoor pool in the country and industry survives in the quarrying of granite and limestone.

The Coast to Coast route leaves the Lake District National Park at Shap. Ahead is limestone country.

Orchid.

SHAP TO KIRKBY STEPHEN

After the excitement of traversing the Lake District the next 20 miles may hold little prospect of visual stimulation. Agreed, the way ahead lacks the drama of mountain and crag, but it does have many fine attributes. The underlying limestone ensures verdant grassland, a wealth of wild flowers and, for the most part, dry paths under foot. Stone circles near Oddendale and Orton, tumuli and ancient dykes testify to the occupation of the area since early times. The Romans built roads here, and modern man has added railways and a motorway. Quarries and ruined limekilns bear witness to former industry and the exploitation of a natural resource.

Robin Hood's Grave.

Limestone country.

A glimpse of the Howgills across Lunedale.

The villages of Ravenstonedale and Newbiggin-on-Lune nestle in the lee of the Howgill fells and provide good accommodation and refreshment.

Smardale Bridge crosses Scandal Beck about a mile and a half north of the village of Ravenstonedale. It dates from the early seventeenth century and, at the Quarter Sessions held at Appleby on 12 April 1602, it was decreed that an assessment of 5d in the pound should be levied on the Bottom of Westmorland for the repair of four bridges of which Smardale was one. Later, in 1649, it was report-

Smardale Bridge and Giants' Graves.

ed to the Assize in Appleby, that sixteen bridges were in a state of decay following the Civil War and a levy of four shillings in the pound should be imposed on the county for their restoration.

Not far from the bridge are conspicuous humps in the ground known locally as giants' graves. The Ordnance Survey prefers to call them pillow mounds. Opinions differ on the origin of these features with some sources saying that they are Bronze Age burial mounds while others hold the view that they are artificial rabbit warrens. *AW* points out that this theory does not hold water, since rabbits were not introudce into this country until the eleventh century. Another theory is that they were platforms for stacking bracken which was used for winter bedding for cattle in previous times. Whatever their use was, it can be safely assumed that they are not the graves of giants.

Further up the valley is the impressive Smardale Gill viaduct, built in 1861 as part of the South Durham and Lancashire Union Railway.

Smardale Gill Viaduct.

The railway was built to carry coke to the blast furnaces of the Cumberland and Furness iron works, iron ore being transported to Cleveland on the return journey. At its height the line carried five passenger trains each week; it was ultimately closed in 1962.

The route ahead climbs steadily between high dry stone walls to cross Smardale Fell affording wide views of the Eden valley and the high Pennines toward Cross Fell.

The Eden valley.

Lime Kiln and, below, Carlisle to Settle Railway.

Small lime kilns like this were in use in this country from medieval times right up to the nineteenth century. They were built wherever fuel (originally wood and later coal or coke) and limestone, could easily be brought together. The fuel and limestone were loaded into the top of the kiln which is why kilns were often built on a hillside for ease of loading. The technique was to add alternate layers of fuel and stone and allow to burn for a week or two, the resultant quick lime was drawn off from the eye at the base of the kiln. As well as its main uses in the buiding industry for the production of mortar and lime wash, it was also used as a fertiliser to sweeten acidic soils. Lime was also used in the tanning and textile industries as well as in soap and papermaking.

After its descent from Smardale Fell, the route crosses the road, passes under the Settle to Carlisle railway, and follows field paths past more ancient settlements to the market town of Kirkby Stephen, the largest community visited so far on the walk. The town's shops, pubs, hotels and B&Bs in abundance are clustered around the Market Square and the twelfth century parish church.

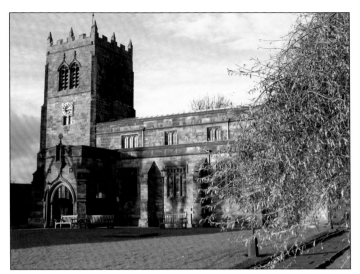

Kirkby Stephen Church and the Loki Stone.

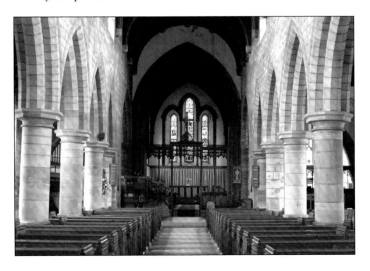

KIRKBY STEPHEN TO KELD

Kirkby Stephen lies at the head of the Eden Valley and, at 600 feet is the highest town on the river. It was granted its market charter by Edward III in 1361 and the market is still held in the square on Mondays. The 'sport' of bull baiting was carried out in the Market Square where cobblestones marked out the bull ring - a practice which continued until 1820 when a bull escaped causing panic among the spectators.

The most imposing building in the town is the parish church, which is known as the Cathedral of the Dales. It dates from 1175 and was built on the site of an earlier

Saxon church. Inside the church, just opposite the door, stands the one metre high Loki Stone, dating from the ninth century. The carved stone portrays Loki, the horned Norse god who caused the death of Odin's son and was imprisoned in chains under ground for his crime. The presence of the stone is testimony to the time when the area was settled by Viking invaders and, as such, is one of the very few surviving physical

reminders of that period in the town's history.

Coast to Coast walkers leave Kirkby Stephen by way of a lane off the Market Square which descends to Frank's Bridge across the infant River Eden. The Eden is Cumbria's longest river with its source high above Mallerstand between Wild Boar Fell and Black Fell Moss where two streams, Red Gill and Little Grain join to form Hell Beck. The river flows roughly northwards towards Appleby-in-Westmorland, gathering water from Cross Fell massif and from Ullswater via the River Eamont, to eventually discharge into the Solway Firth near Carlisle, almost 100 miles from its source.

Field paths and a short lane lead to the picturesque village of Hartley where the fell road is joined, passing Merrygill viaduct and Hartly Quarry to Fell House where the road ends and the ascent of Nine Standards Rigg begins.

Above, a view of Kirkby Stephen and, right, Frank's Bridge.

The road climbs steeply between banks of gorse and arrives at a splendid seat erected to the memory of Brian Saunders from which fine retrospective views of the Eden Valley can be enjoyed with the high Pennines beyond. The character of the walk changes again here. Just as the hard rock terrain of the Lake District gave way to the milder limestone scenery around Shap, the way ahead lies over typical Pennine country where peat and bog predominate. Heather, cotton grass and rushes prevail and provide cover for red grouse, curlew and golden plover which make their home here.

Above, Hartley, and below the Eden Valley looking towards Cross Fell.

Heather burning on Hartley Fell.

The approach to the Nine Standards.

Nine Standards.

Beacons, boundary markers, pseudo-castles to fool the marauding Scots, ore merely just built for something to do? Theories of the origin of the Standards are legion.

Whatever their *raison d'être* they have been here for centuries occupying this commanding position above the Eden Valley.

70

Erosion caused by the boots of thousands of walkers has taken its toll on the paths to Nine Standards Rigg. To minimise further damage, three routes are in place and are used at different times of the year. The routes also take into account the needs of ground nesting birds and conse-quently, at some times of year, certain parts of the fell should be avoided. The red and blue routes traverse the fell, while the green route avoids it altogether and skirts Dukerdale to join the B6270 road near Tailbrigg Pots.

The routes converge at the bottom of Ney Gill where a

Towards White Mossy Hill.

narrow tarmac road leads to Raven Seat a farm surrounded by wild flower meadows, which lies in a fold in the hills by the side of Whitsundale Beck.

Limestone re-appears at the cliff of Cotterby Scar which constrains the River Swale and provides an impressive back drop to Wain Wath Force. The road shares the valley bottom with the Swale to arrive in Keld half a mile further on.

Raven Seat.

Wain Wath Force and Cotterby Scar.

Above, Keld and below Hoggarts Leap

KELD TO REETH

Keld is a tiny village which sits on the edge of a deep, tree-lined, limestone gorge occupied by the River Swale. It is significant on the Coast to Coast walk in that it is the first Yorkshire village visited and also it marks the halfway point. The village is a magnet for tourists who come to walk the riverside paths and to visit the tea room. There is a camp site and a car park. *AW* says: 'Always, at Keld, there is the music of the river' and he could not be more correct.

For a lover of waterfalls and riverside scenery Keld is a wonderful place. However, some of the falls are more accessible than others. Hoggarts Leap is easily visited after a short walk across the camp site, as is the top of Catrake Force, but a visit to the bottom of the force is a far more serious proposition, one which this writer failed to accomplish. A local resident said there used to be a stairway behind the farm buildings which led down to the river but this is long gone - perhaps *AW* used it when he produced his drawing of the waterfall.

East Gill Force and Kisdown Force are downstream of Keld, the latter being approached by taking a left turn from the riverside path to Muker and passing below some crags to skirt the thickly wooded hillside before descending to river level.

There is a choice of routes from Keld to Reeth

and they are as different as chalk from cheese, though both leave the village via a muddy lane on the right bank of the river. The first route follows footpaths through beautiful scenery along or close to the Swale through Muker, Gunnerside and Feetham. The other option is a high level route following miners' tracks over rough moorland. Here beauty is in short supply due to the devastation caused by lead mining. The mines are long abandoned but sufficient remains to stimulate the imaginaton and speculate on the lives of the thousands of men who won their livings in these harsh surroundings.

Left, East Gill Force and above, East Gill beck joins the Swale.

Kisdon Force.

From the gated footbridge over the Swale the track, shared by the Pennine Way for a short distance, ascends the hillside and crosses East Gill just above the waterfall.

A pleasantly rising, well-surfaced path leads across the fell side to arrive at the ruins of Crackpot Hall. Even less of this once proud farmhouse remains than is shown in

The Swale below Keld.

Swaledale.

Above, the track from Keld and below the ruins of Crackpot Hall

AW's drawing of the scene, but the view downstream towards Muker, can have changed little since then or indeed from the time when the farm was occupied.

Beyond Crackpot Hall the character of the walk changes abruptly. The pastoral beauty of the valley is left behind (at least temporarily) and a landscape scarred by centuries of lead mining is entered. Although lead ore has been extracte here, and in neighbouring Arkengarthdale since Roman times, most of the mines date from the seventeenth and eighteenth centuries. The industry thrived and, over the years, employed thousands of men until the latter half of the nineteenth century. By this time most of the best veins had been fully exploited and cheaper imported material was being used to supply the home market. The mines and smelt mills were abandoned and Swaledale suffered a dramatic decline in population. For some there would have been a transition from mining to farming, but many more were forced to leave the area perhaps to continue their mining skills in the coal fields of County Durham.

The Swinnergill mines complex with its levels and ruined smelt house is the first to be encountered after leaving Crackpot Hall.

The route climbs out of Swinner Gill and crosses heather moorland to arrive at the edge of Gunnerside Gill which conceals the remains of Bunton Mines in its depths.

After crossing Gunnerside Beck the path

Swinner Gill.

The bridge, Swinner Gill.

Looking down Swinner Gill.

Ruins of Swinnergill Smelt Mill complete with dressed stone doorway.

follows the eastern side of the gill before branching off to the left across an area where the devastation is absolute.

Not even hardy moorland vegetation can gain any foothold here, the whole of the fell top being covered with

Gunnerside Gill.

a thick layer of gravel, the remains of the spoil heaps of Old Gang Mines. Rusting machinery adds to the general desolation and incongruously, a line of grouse butts cross-es the path as it descends alongside a ruined wall to Level House Bridge.

Slightly higher and to the left of the track can be seen

Bunton Mine.

the remains of the peat store which supplied fuel to the smelt mill below. The building, which was thatched with heather, is 117 metres long by 6.3 metres wide and, reput-edly, could hold sufficient fuel to keep the mill going for three years.

Level House Bridge.

The photograph opposite was taken on a cold blustery day in early May. As I sheltered from the wind in a corner of the furnace house and lit my pipe, it was easy to imagine the atmosphere when the mill was in full production. Heat, noise, the smell of burning peat and hot metal, shouts, curses, the good natured ribbing meted out to any-one who merited it would have combined to form an *esprit de corps* that only exists where men are working together in dangerous occupations.

A wide track leads from Old Gang to join the main road at Surrender Bridge where another smelt mill can be found.

Old Gang peat store.

Old Gang Smelt Mill.

Surrender Bridge.

The way ahead crosses a deep ravine, Cringley Bottom, skirts the lower slopes of Calver Hill and follows field paths for the next three miles to arrive in Reeth, the captial of upper Swaledale.

Calver Hill and Surrender Bridge Smelt Mill.

Reeth.

Reeth is a busy market town situated at the junction of Swaledale and Arkengarthdale. Once primarly concerned with the administration of the mining industry, Reeth is now centre for tourists whose needs are catered for by the many hostelries and cafés which surround its large green. There has been a settlement here since Saxon times which expanded enough following the Norman conquest for it to be included in the Doomsday Book. Reeth is something of a milestone on the Coast to Coast walk in that it marks the end of a high level traverse; it's all downhill now until the Cleveland Hills, well nearly!

REETH TO RICHMOND

After the austerity of the journey from Keld amid the decaying remains of a long dead industry, the next ten miles offers scenery of unsurpassed tranquility. The way ahead broadly follows the course of the Swale, which having left its torrent section far behind, now occupies a wide river valley. Quiet public and farm roads lead in due course to Marrick Priory which was founded as a Benedictine nunnery in 1154 and dissolved in 1539. The priory is now in ruins except for the tower and is partly hidden by new buildings which house an activity and adventure centre.

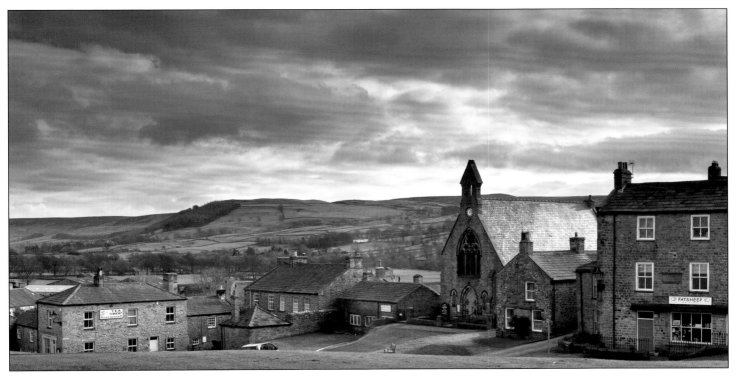

Reeth.

Marrick Priory.

Two miles beyond Marrick Priory in a sylvan setting by the side of the beck to which it gives its name, lives the estate village of Marske. Marske Hall, built by the Hutton family in 1597, and occupied by them for centuries, stands in landscaped grounds at the entrance to the village.

Marske Hall.

Marske Church.

Nearby is the twelfth century parish church dedicated to St. Edmund the martyr. Patronage of the church by the Hutton farmily began in 1598 when the then Archbishop of York, Matthew Hutton, purchased the estate. The Hutton family can claim the distinction of being unique in providing two Archbishops, both called Matthew, the first becoming Archbishop of York in 1595 and the second Archbishop of York in 1747 and Canterbury in 1757.

Yet another Matthew Hutton, not a churchman this time but a captain in the army, is commemorated by a 60 foot obelisk erected after his death in 1813 to mark his grave at a place where, as a boy, he loved to sit and admire the view.

The Coast to Coask walk leaves Marske by the Richmond road and after branching right across pasture land and Clapgate Beck, arrives at a cairn where the path meets the farm road to West Applegarth. The limestone cliff which accompanies the track is Applegarth Scar. The road comes to an end at West Applegarth and the path continues across fields and over one or two awkward stiles before joining another 'road' close to East Applegarth farm. The track ascends the slope beneath Whitcliffe Scar to enter Whitcliffe Wood passing grassy banks which are thickly carpeted by primroses in spring.

Looking back towards Marske and below Applegarth Scar.

Spring primroses.

East Applegarth, below Whitcliffe Scar, and right, Whitcliffe Wood.

The road ahead leads into Richmond with its Norman castle set high above the River Swale. Although there has been a settlement here since Saxon times, there seems to have been no fortification until after the Norman Conquest. The building of the castle started in 1071 on land given to Alan the Red from Brittany by William the

Richmond Castle.

The Keep.

Castle Walk.

Holy Trinity Church and below Culloden Tower and Georgian Theatre extension.

Conqueror as a reward for his help in defeating in King Harold.

The medieval Holy Trinity Church in the Market Place is now the military museum of the Green Howard's regiment. A little way out of town and best viewed from Castle Walk, stands Culloden Tower. It was built as a folly in 1746 by John Yorke, Richmond's MP, to mark the defeat of the Scots at Culloden Moor and the establishment of Hanoverian rule. Inside are two tall octagonal rooms, one above the other, which contain high quality carvings and plaster work.

Richmond's Georgian Theatre has enjoyed a chequered history. It was built in 1788 and in use for about 60 years, closing in 1848 and was then

let as an auction room. It reopened in 1963 and was extensively renovated in 2003.

Opposite the Georgian Theatre in the Friary Memorial Gardens stands one of Richmond's most historic monu-

Greyfriars Tower.

ments. The Friary Tower was built in the fifteenth century by the Grey Friars of Richmond as part of an expansion of the Franciscan Friary first established in 1257 on land donated by Ralf Fitz Randal, Lord of Middleham. Major restoration work on the tower was completed in 2003 allowing increased public accessibility.

Thus Richmond has an impressive history only touched on here. Neolithic flints and Iron Age earthworks built by the Brigantes have been discovered nearby. Pottery and a hoard of silver coins and spoons found at Castle Bank attest to Roman occupation and a Viking sword with a silver hilt was discovered at Gilling West.

The Market Place, complete with stocks and a pillory for the punishment of miscreants, was laid down in medieval times and the town suffered an attack of bubonic plague in 1349. John Wesley preached here in 1768, while on one of his evangelical tours of northern England, and Lewis Carroll (Charles Dodgson) who went on to write *Alice in Wonderland* attended Richmond Grammar School whose roots lie in Elizabethan times.

Restoration of the theatre and the Friary Tower have already been mentioned, but the story does not end there. In recent times the railway station, a victim of cuts in the 1960s, has been refurbished to provide an art gallery, a cinema and a restaurant. A micro-brewery as well as ice cream and cheese making facilities have been established, and rooms are available for private and community use. All of this, together with the magnificent Swaledale scenery, make Richmond a place to savour.

Waterfalls at Richmond.

RICHMOND TO INGLEBY CROSS

Quaint cobbled streets lead off the Market Place a nd descend steeply to Richmond Bridge which *AW* recommends as the exit from Richmond. Here begins what he describes as, "a tedious crossing of the Vale of Mowbray devoid of interest to lovers of wild places." However, the first couple of miles can be enlivened by following the Drummer Boy Walk along the banks of the River Swale through Flint Bank Wood to Easby Abbey.

Legend has it that in medieval times a tunnel was constructed connecting Easby Abbey to Richmond Castle to provide an escape route for the White Canons in the event of an attack by the Scots. At the end of the eighteenth century soldiers discovered the partly collapsed entrance to the tunnel beneath the Castle Keep and, because the passage was very narrow, enlisted the services of a little drummer boy to enter the tunnel. He was instructed to beat his drum so that the soldiers on the surface could follow his progress and chart the route of the underground passage. The sound led them across the Market Place, down Frenchgate and along the banks of the Swale into Easby Wood where, about half a mile from the Abbey, the

Richmond Bridge and right The Drummer Boy Stone.

drumming suddenly stopped. Some sources embellish the tale further, and claim that the boy met King Arthur and his knights slumbering in a cavern until needed to defend the shores of England, and he elected to stay with them. The boy was never seen again, but a stone marks the place where the drumming ceased.

To follow the Drummer Boy Walk, leave the Market Place via Frenchgate, and follow Station Road to a lane just past St. Mary's Church where the path to Easby Abbey is well marked if rather muddy. Continue past the

Easby Abbey.

Easby Abbey.

abbey and cross the River Swale by means of an old iron railway bridge to rejoin Wainwright's route.

Easby Abbey and the nearby parish church are dedicated to St. Agatha the patron saint of sufferers of diseases of the breast and protector against fire. The latter association is due to the mode of her martyrdom - she was exposed to flames but not permitted to be burned to death - instead she was taken to a dungeon to die in agony. The breast disease connection is because it was ordered that her breasts be torn off by slaves with iron pincers.

The abbey was founded in about 1152 by the Premonstratensians who came to be known as the White Canons due to the colour of their habits. The monks were in constant fear of attack from the Scots and were forced to beg protection from the English Army. Unfortunately this proved disastrous. In 1346 an army en route to the battle of Nevilles Cross was billeted in the abbey and, in a drunken orgy of destruction, caused more damage than the Scots would ever have done. The abbey was abandoned at the time of the Dissolution.

The route continues on a succession of field paths and farm tracks to Colburn and then along the wooded banks of the River Swale to Catterick Bridge. Cataractonium, from which Catterick takes its name, was a Roman town founded in 70AD to keep the revolutionary Brigantes in check. Today it is most notable for its army base and for its racecourse.

Catterick Bridge.

The way ahead follows the river until a gravel works forces a diversion on to the B6271; fenced lanes lead to Bolton-on-Swale with St. Mary's Church visible amongst the trees. St. Mary's Church is in the Gothic style and dates from the first half of fourteenth century. The site was previously occupied by both Saxon and Norman churches, remains of both being incorporated into the present building. Notable in the churchyard is a

St. Mary's Church, Bolton-on-Swale.

The Jenkins Memorial.

monument erected in 1743 by public contribution to commemorate the long life of Henry Jenkins who was born at Elerton-on-Swale in the year 1500 and died there in 1670 at the age of 169 years! He pursued his employment as a fisherman for 140 years and, according to local lore, regularly swam across the Swale, even he was over 100-years-old.

Uneventful walking through an agricultural landscape leads to Danby Wiske which Wainwright unkindly describes as a 'slough of despond.' Not even the promised bag of crisps was available when I visited as the pub was being refurbished; the church too was being renovated.

Between Danby Wiske and Ingleby Cross the route follows the road initially, crossing the main east coast railway close to the former railway station, and continues along Danby Lane to Oaktree Hill. Close by is the site of

Danby Wiske Parish Church.

the Battle of the Standard fought in 1138 between the Scots and an army gathered by Thurstan, the then Archbishop of York. Amongst this force were the city militias of York, Beverly and Ripon who marched under their religious banners or standards which bore the symbols of the patron saints of each city, St Peter, St John and St Wilfred respectively. It was these standards which eventually gave the battle its title. Further lanes and field paths lead past Sydal Lodge to Ingleby Arncliffe and thence to Ingleby Cross and the Blue Bell Inn.

The Blue Bell Inn.

Ingleby Arncliffe Church.

INGLEBY CROSS TO CLAY BANK TOP

Arrival at Ingleby Cross should be an occasion for celebration. Finally the long trudge across the Vale of Mowbray is at an end and ahead lies a traverse of the North York Moors. This is a land of high moorland clad in heather and bilberry, wooded valleys, rocky outcrops and picturesque villages. The walker is well served with excellent footpaths and quiet roads.

Those interested in historical remains will be rewarded with ancient cairns, barrows and earthworks, while botanists and geologists are well catered for in this varied landscape. The district was formerly exploited for its mineral wealth; coal, jet and alum were mined here and it was the discovery or iron ore in the area which led to the birth of Middlesbrough as a major industrial centre and port. All is quiet now - mineral extraction has ceased and nature is reclaiming the abandoned railways, quarries and spoil heaps which testify to the region's industrial past.

From the Blue Bell the way ahead leads over the busy A172 Thirsk to Stokesley road and up the lane towards the church and Arncliffe Hall, which were once surrounded by a moat, the remains of which can still be traced. The church of All Saints is in Gothic style with high pointed sash windows and was built in 1821 to replace an earlier building, the east window of the early church being incorporated into the present structure.

Arncliffe Hall, built in 1754 by John Carr of York, replaces a sixteenth century house on the same site.

Behind the hall, the ground rises steeply through Arncliffe Wood to the summit of Beacon Hill which provides extensive views of the way ahead.

Nearby in a wooded setting stands Mount Grace Priory. Dating from 1398, this is one of the best remaining examples of a Carthusian foundation where monks

The Church, Mount Grace Priory.

lived a solitary existence in individual cells, each with its own small garden.

The path climbs through Arncliffe Wood and emerges near an abandoned quarry to follow a dry stone wall and pass a British Telecom microwave relay station of 'revolting appearance' according to Wainwright. The sharp-eyed will notice the verse fixed to the information board inside the perimeter fence:

> *Be ye man or be ye woman*
> *Be ye going or be ye comin'*
> *Be ye soon or be ye late*
> *Be ye sure to shut this gate*

Ascribed to Ripon CS School, the verse once adorned a gate on Beacon Hill. The summit is unremarkable, the OS column standing in a flat field, but the view is extensive.

Above, Beacon Hill Summit, below, Arncliffe Wood and right, British Telecom Station.

Descent from Beacon Hill.

Carlton Moor across Scarth Nick, Whorl Hill and Roseberry Topping in the distance.

The Ford in Scugdale and below, Carlton Moor.

The path descends from the Ordnance column alongside the wall on the edge of Scarth Wood, passes through a gate and continues across the heather of Scarth Wood Moor. The stone wall is rejoined a little further on and leads down steeply to cross the Swainby to Osmotherly road through Scarth Nick at a cattle grid. A traverse of the wooded slopes of Coalmire leads to a gentle descent into the charming valley of Scugdale, where evidence of former mining activity can still be discerned.

Scugdale Beck is crossed at a ford, or by the footbridge if you want to keep your boots dry, and the lane leads to Huthwaite Green. The path leaves Huthwaite Green and rises steeply at first to cross the heather clad slopes of Live Moor and Holey Moot to arrive at the boundary stone and Ordnance column on the summit of Carleton Moor. A line of pink spoil heaps lower down on the slopes of Carleton Moor testifies to an industrial past of jet mining and the top of the fell bears the scars of runways formerly used by a local gliding club. Gliding activity seems to have stopped but hang gliders taking off from lower down the hill are a common sight at weekends.

The bulk of Cringle Moor, the next objective on the Coast to Coast walk dominates the view to the east, but the panorama is extensive in other directions. The high Pennines including Cross Fell in the west are visible on a clear day, while the foreground is occupied by the valley of the River Tees and the industrial conurbation of Teesside guarded by the proud little peak of Roseberry Topping.

Boundary stone and Ordnance Column on Carlton Moor.

Cringle Moor from the old alum workings on Carlton Moor.

The paved path descends steeply from the summit of Carlton Moor to cross the Carlton to Chop Gate road at Carlton Bank where hang-gliding enthusiasts can be seen launching themselves into space. Across the road, the way lies over a flat grassy field and accompanies a stone wall to the promontory of Cringle End, then follows the edge of the escarpment towards the summit of the fell, which is marked by a cairn on a tumulus. Cringle Moor at 435 metres is the highest point reached so far on the North Yorkshire Moors section of the walk and is only over topped by Round Hill at 454 metres, on Urra Moor.

Seat and view indicator on Cringle End.

Cairn on Tumulus, summit of Cringle Moor.

Looking back to Cringle Moor from Cold Moor.

The next summit on this switchback ridge is Cold Moor. A mile distant and only 33 metres lower than Cringle Moor, its ascent involves a loss and subsequent retrieval of just over 120 metres in altitude.

Cold Moor from Cringle Moor.

There is a similar depression between Cold Moor and Hasty Bank, but this time there is added interest in the form of the Wainstones which Wainwright describes as, 'a cluster of fanged and pinnacled rocks.' I can't better his description.

The Wainstones.

Towards Bilsdale.

The traverse of Hasty Bank is a pleasure; a well paved path leads through heather and bilberry on an airy ridge. Ahead can be seen the next stage of the walk on Urra Moor and retrospective views are a reward for the effort so far expended.

Looking back to Cold Moor and Cringle Moor from Hasty Bank.

Carr Ridge and Urra Moor from Hasty Bank.

Hasty Bank, the approach to Carr Ridge and Roseberry Topping.

CLAY BANK TOP TO GLAISDALE

The route descends the flank of Hasty Bank to cross the B1257 road at the entrance to Bilsdale and passes through Haggs Gate before beginning the climb to Carr Ridge and Urra Moor. The well-paved path through banks of bilberry follows a stone wall steeply upwards. In summer it's wonderful, when the sun shines, the larks sing and the cattle graze contentedly. There are fine views of Bilsdale below and the Hasty Bank to Cringle Moor ridge in retrospect. Can this idyll continue until Glaisdale? Unfortunately, the answer is no. As the gradient eases a vast tract of heather moor, a landscape that only a grouse could find attractive, comes into view. To be fair though, for three or four weeks in late summer, when the heather is in bloom it looks spectacular.

Bilsdale.

Despite my unkind remarks, Urra Moor is not to be missed. Tumuli, burial mounds and carved stones bear witness to long vanished civilisations and its summit, Round Hill at 454 metres (1489 feet) is the highest point on the Cleveland Hills.

Among the many boundary and standing stones on Urra Moor is the Hand stone which is close to the Ordnance Survey column on Round Hill. Way markers, in the form of cairns or more decorative monoliths have been erected since ancient times to guide travellers across featureless terrain. Though barely discernable, the Hand Stone is inscribed, "This way to KIR (Kirkbymoorside)"

Hasty Bank, Cold Moor and Cringle Moor from Urra Moor.

The Hand Stone and OS column on Round Hill.

and "This way to STOXLA (Stokesley)."

The old road across the moor descends slightly over Cockayne Head to Bloworth Crossing on the track of the former Rosedale Ironstone Railway. The railway was dismantled in 1929 but its course, which is followed for the next six miles across Farndale and High Blakey Moors, enables rapid progress to be made.

Ironstone has been mined in the Cleveland Hills for centuries, perhaps since Roman times but did not achieve commercial viability until the latter half of the nineteenth century when mining began in earnest at Hollins Farm close to Rosedale Abbey. Initially, mining was by open-cast methods which were soon replaced by adits and shafts sunk into the hillsides.

Towards Bloworth Crossing from Cockayne Head.

Blakey Junction and below, Rosedale.

The increased production of ore rendered the previous method of transportation, horse drawn carts to the rail-head at Pickering, inadequate and necessitated the construction of a railway to carry the ironstone to the blast furnaces of the burgeoning town of Middlesbrough. The original line, which was opened in 1861, began at Bank Top on the western side of Rosedale and was joined in 1865 by a branch line from the eastern mines at Blakey Junction. From here the railway crossed the high moors and descended to Ingleby Botton, by means of a mile long incline with a maximum gradient of one in five to connect to the main rail network at Battersby Junction.

Construction of the line was a major feat of engineering. Although many watersheds and valleys were crossed, no bridges or tunnels were built and an almost level course on the 1,300 foot contour was maintained by the use of cuttings and embankments.

The Lion Inn on Blakey Ridge dates from 1553 and stands in splendid isolation on the Castleton to

Rosedale Railway, below, Farndale and right, the Lion Inn.

Hutton-le-Hole road. You can get a bed for the night here (but you might have to book six months in advance) and good food and drink. It is a gladsome sight after the desolation of the moorland crossing but don't get too excited about this return to civilisation, there is still another seven miles of heather to cross before the descent into Glaisdale! Leaving the Lion Inn behind, the route continues along the road to a boundary stone (Margery Bradley) where a path branches off to the right towards the conspicuous White Cross, otherwise known as Fat Betty. Alternatively, the road can be followed to a junction and the road to Rosedale Abbey taken to arrive at the cross. Nearby are the

Clockwise, Young Ralph Cross, Fat Betty and Elgee memorial.

Trough House and below the Big Cairn on Glaisdale Rigg.

Ralph Crosses and the Frank Elgee memorial.

Frank Elgee was a renowned naturalist and archaeologist who conducted a number of important excavations in the 1920s and 1930s. His research into early settlements on the North Yorkshire moors received national acclaim. The stone is simply inscribed, 'Frank Elgee 1880-1944.'

A little further along the road is the Young Ralph Cross whose image has been used as the symbol of the North Yorkshire Moors National Park since 1974. There has been a cross, originally wooden, on this site since the thirteenth century; the present structure probably dates from the eighteenth century. Legend has it that the body of a tramp was discovered on this spot by Ralph, a farmer from Danby, who erected the cross as a guide post for future travellers. About 200 metres west of Young Ralph and not seen from the route is Old Ralph Cross which marks the division of the parishes of Esklets, Westerdale and Rosedale.

Fat Betty also marks the junction of three parishes, namely Danby, Westerdale and Rosedale. The head of the cross is a wheelhead, one of only two in the area and is believed to date from Norman times. It may take its name from Sister Elizabeth, a nun from nearby Rosedale Abbey. This was a Cistercian order whose members wore undyed woollen clothing and were known as the White Ladies. Another legend is that a farmer's wife, fat Betty, fell from her horse and cart on the moor. When she failed to return home the farmer searched for her but only found a large, fat stone.

Glaisdale Church.

From Fat Betty the route follows the road for a little over a mile before branching off across the moor to pass by Trough House, a lunch hut for grouse shooting parties. An area of old coal pits is passed and Glaisdale Moor traversed before joining the Lealholm to Rosedale Abbey road a little way from the 'Big Cairn' on Glaisdale Rigg. The track across Glaisdale Rigg, once known as Whitby Road, leads down into the village where the church, dedicated to Saint Thomas, occupies a vantage point looking up to Glaisdale Head and the moors beyond. The way ahead follows the road past the railway station before crossing a footbridge to enter East Arncliffe Wood close to Beggars Bridge, which was built by Thomas Ferris who came to the district as a tramp and vowed that, if he could ever afford it, he would build a bridge to replace the stepping stones which saved him in a time of flood.

Beggars Bridge.

St. Hedda's Church, Egton Bridge.

GLAISDALE TO ROBIN HOOD'S BAY

This final section of the walk has something for everyone. Whether your preference is for riverside walks, enchanting woodland, heather moors, waterfalls, picturesque villages, cliff top paths or even steam locomotives, the last nineteen miles cannot fail to delight. The path leaves East Arnecliff Wood and enters Egton Bridge, a small village built in pleasantly wooded countryside on the banks of the River Esk. The jewel in the crown is the Roman Catholic Church, built in 1860 and dedicated to Saint Hedda, a seventh century monk educated at nearby Whitby, who became Bishop of Winchester. Externally the church has a fine apse and coloured panels in bas-relief depicting episodes from the scriptures. The sumptuous interior is more reminiscent of southern Italy than the North Yorkshire moors.

Egton Bridge is left by a footpath along the private estate road of Egton Manor. The present house, built in the eighteenth century, occupies the site of a former thirteenth century manor house. After about a mile the private road joins the Egton road which crosses the bridge over the Esk on the outskirts of Grosmont (pronounced Gro-mont) and passes playing fields to enter the village. While Glaisdale and Egton Bridge are served by the railway, here a group of enthusiasts, the North York Moors Railway Society, preserve the line, one of George Stephenson's creations, and operate a service with steam locomotives on the Pickering to Whitby line.

Above, bridge over the Esk and below, steam engine at Grosmont.

The Old Mill Littlebeck.

Passage over the railway at the level crossing may involve a considerable wait if it is a steam festival weekend. Here steam takes precedence over all other traffic, engines are shunted back and forth, and the gates remain closed. The road rises steeply through the village and reaches the open moor close to Low and High Bride Stones. Flat Howe, a tumulus, is close by and it is from here that the North Sea with Whitby, and its abbey in the foreground, first come into view. A bridleway leaves the main Pickering to Whitby road and leads downhill to join a lane which enters the charming hamlet of Littlebeck. The beck is crossed at a ford and around a bend in the road, a footpath through the wood signposted 'Falling Foss' is followed, passing old spoil heaps and an enormous boulder hollowed out to provide a shelter, complete

Falling Foss.

The Hermitage.

with seats and inscribed 'The Hermitage, 1790.'

The path through the wood is easily followed but is muddy and slippery after rain. It joins a network of paths forming a forest trail around the Foss. The waterfall, in its sylvan setting, is magical. Unfortunately access to the bottom of the falls is prevented by fencing (it would be an uncomfortable descent anyway) and so the view as depicted in Wainwright's drawing is not available. The route continues from the car park, initially following the road before crossing Sneaton Low Moor and the B1416 to Graystone Hills from where a lane leads on to the road two miles from Hawsker. The village is in two parts, High and Low, and boasts a good pub providing much needed refreshment.

The inclusion of Hawsker on the Coast to Coast walk

involves a considerable detour fom the direct route to Robin Hood's Bay which is only two miles distant along the B1447 from its junction with the main Scarborough to Whitby road.

As *AW* says, "you could be there, licking ice cream and eyeing the girls, in half an hour, mission accomplished..." The reason for rejecting this easier option is that to take it would miss out on the coastal path along the top of the cliffs with its magnificent views. Hawsker is left by the road which climbs out of the village, a lane on the left gives acess to what *AW* calls Seaview and Northcliffe 'caravan sites'! He could probably be had under the trades descriptions act these days. The holiday accommodation found here did not arrive being towed by a Ford Mondeo, only an articulated lorry with a 40 foot trailer would be man enough for the task.

The lane continues downhill and crosses Oakham Beck close to the tourist information centre and enters the Northcliffe site, which provides access to the coastal path, part of the Cleveland Way, at Maw Wyke Hole. The cliff scenery is spectacular and there is no difficulty in route finding here, simply turn right and don't stray too far to the left! Robin Hood's Bay is two miles further on but coyly keeps hidden until its revelation at Ness Point.

Hawsker.

Maw Wyke Hole.

Robin Hood's Bay.

So here it is, the promised land, Robin Hood's Bay seen across the rooftops of Bay Town. Three National Parks and 190 miles from the start point at St. Bees and the culmination of perhaps two weeks of walking through the best scenery that the North of England has to offer.

Only one duty remains, the steep ascent of Station Road into Bay Town and the ritual anointing of the boots in the North Sea.

The quaint, historic, streets of this one time small fishing village, formerly the haunt of excise dodging

The Bay Hotel.

Bay Town.

smugglers, is today a popular tourist centre. Hotels, restaurants and cafés abound to cater for the influx of visitors, and shops sell traditional craft goods alongside the usual seaside paraphernalia. Fortunately, here it is not the case that the tourist has destroyed the scene he came to see, and the atmosphere is still that of a picturesque village tucked away between the rocky headlands which rise to either side of it. Wainwright says that you can now rest on your laurels and enjoy a pint in the Bay Hotel, and so you can, but over indulgence is not recommended; remember it's an awfully big climb back up to Station Road!

Ennerdale from Haystacks and below, Glenridding.

IN CONCLUSION

Everyone who completes the Coast to Coast walk will take away with them memories of favourite sections of the expedition and probably no two lists of the highlights will tally. The following is a personal selection of what I consider to be the best bits. The Lake District is firmly established as supreme walking country but, in my opinion (he said putting on his flak jacket), the Coast to Coast doesn't visit the most spectacular parts of the region.

The walk up Ennerdale is tedious and the excitement does not begin until the valley is left behind and the open fell around Haystacks is reached. If the walk started at Ravenglass or Seasale, and followed Eskdale or Wasdale onto the Scafell massif and then descended to Borrowdale via Sty Head Pass, this section of the journey would provide, in my opinion, more interest. Of course, if that were the case, the distinction of starting and finishing on a cliff top would be lost so perhaps I should stop moaning and just accept that hindsight is a cheap commodity and that thousands of people have enjoyed the walk just as it is.

The photographs in this book were taken in 2009-10 when the weather was not kind - the summer was poor and the winter horrendous. Several sections in the Lakes yielded no useable pictures and resulted in one or two omissions which I regret. In particular I wanted to include Striding Edge on Helvellyn but snow, ice and the state of my legs prevented this particular visit.

Above, Haweswater and below Shap Abbey.

The inclusion of Haweswater in a list of favourites may come as a surprise to many, and it is true that when the reservoir is drawn down and the shoreline is exposed, it is not a pretty sight. However, when the lake is full and the sun is shining the scene is captivating.

I had never visited Shap Abbey before embarking on this walk, but found it an idyllic spot. The historic ruin nestling in its pastoral setting by the banks of the River Lowther presents a scene of rural tranquility.

Smardale, lying between the Howgill Fells and the Eden Valley was another happy discovery. The luxuriant green of the grassland is due to the underlying limestone which promotes the growth of a rich variety of many types of grasses and flowers.

Left, Smardale Gill, above Scandal Beck and below the Vale of Eden.

Old Gang Smelt Mill, below, Lower East Gill Force, and to the right, Muker Church.

Much of Upper Swaledale has been scarred by the lead mining industry, but the abandoned workings are a source of great interest. Elsewhere the countryside is charming. Swaledale is definitely one of the best sections.

Waterfalls on the Swale, Hasty Bank and North Sea Cliffs.

Robin Hood's Bay.

I said at the beginning of this final section that everyone would have their own list of favourite places and that probably no two lists would be the same. I've just looked back on the last few pages and thought, yes these are fine but what about the view down the Buttermere Valley or the Nine Standards, the vista from Cringle End or the first sight of Robin Hood's Bay from the cliff top path.

The truth is that it's all good and trying to pick the best bits from a 190-mile journey is too hard a task. As someone once said 'comparisons are odourous.' I hope that the photographs in this book will bring back happy memories to readers who have completed the walk, and inspire those who have yet to do so, to put their boots on and give it a try. If you do, I'm sure you'll have an interesting time.

Nine Standards.

Safety on the Hills

Wainwright says in his book Fellwanderer: "Fell walking accidents happen only to those who walk clumsily. The only advice you need (and this shouldn't be necessary either) is to 'watch where you are putting your feet.'" Well yes, but perhaps this needs a little clarification. The summit of Haystacks or Striding Edge are not inherently dangerous places but Striding Edge in a howling gale or when the rocks are covered in ice is extremely dangerous; discretion always needs to be exercised on the choice of route with regard to prevailing weather conditions.

Wainwright's choice of clothing was biased towards Harris Tweed, and why not? However, modern light weight warm clothing is perhaps more suitable for those following the Coast to Coast walk. You probably won't die from exposure if you get soaked on Urra Moor but the Lion Inn is eight uncomfortable miles away so a set of waterproofs in the rucksack is a good idea. *AW* was an ardent admirer of the Ordnance Survey and there is no doubt that its publications together with a compass and the ability to use them are essential in wild places. A mobile phone may get you out of trouble if you get lost, a map and compass will prevent you from getting lost in the first place!

There are some fairly long sections on the walk and pubs and cafés are few and far between so don't forget the needs of the inner person and pack enough food and drink to last the day. Also, it is always good to let someone know your planned route so, if you don't arrive at your destination in the evening, the alarm will be raised.

The cliff top path on the approach to Robin Hood's Bay is, in places, very close to the edge, definitely watch where you're putting your feet here!

The Coast to Coast walk is a pleasure trip not a military route march, the following will add to the pleasure without adding too much to the baggage:

Adequate outdoor clothing and waterproofs
Comfortable, well broken in boots
Maps and a compass
Small first-aid kit
LED torch (so you can see where you're putting your feet in the dark)
Mobile phone
Sun bloc (hopefully)

Have a safe trip.

Also by David Shaw, *Teesdale in Pictures*
(ISBN 1904524591) available direct from bookshops or from
Hayloft Publishing Ltd at: www.hayloft.eu